Contents

D0111924

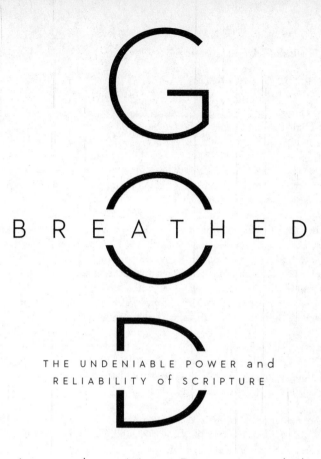

GOD BREATHED

THE UNDENIABLE POWER and RELIABILITY of SCRIPTURE

Josh McDowell

STUDY GUIDE
FOR INDIVIDUALS AND ADULT GROUPS

SHILOH RUN PRESS

An Imprint of Barbour Publishing, Inc.

© 2015 by Josh McDowell Ministry

Print ISBN 978-1-63058-944-8

eBook Editions:
Adobe Digital Edition (.epub) 978-1-63409-383-5
Kindle and MobiPocket Edition (.prc) 978-1-63409-384-2

Cover design: Faceout Studio, faceoutstudio.com

Published by Shiloh Run Press, an imprint of Barbour Publishing, Inc., P.O. Box 719, Uhrichsville, Ohio 44683, www.shilohrunpress.com.

Our mission is to publish and distribute inspirational products offering exceptional value and biblical encouragement to the masses.

 Member of the
Evangelical Christian
Publishers Association

Printed in the United States of America.

Acknowledgments

I would like to thank those people who helped make this study guide a reality:

Dave Bellis, my friend and colleague for more than thirty-seven years, for collaborating with me in writing *God-Breathed* and for writing this study guide. I recognize Dave's insights and talents in developing these kinds of group study guides, and I'm grateful for his contribution.

Becky Bellis, for laboring at the computer to prepare the manuscript for this study guide.

Kelly McIntosh and *Tim Martins* of Barbour Publishing, for their vision and passion to provide the body of Christ with this study tool so they might more deeply experience the God-breathed truths of Scripture.

Josh McDowell

How to Get the Most Out of This Study Experience

This five-session *God-Breathed Study Guide* is to be used by small groups or can be used for individual study. While you can answer the questions throughout this guide from your own knowledge and the Scripture references given, you will get the most out of this experience if you read *God-Breathed*, the companion book to this study. If this study is used within a group, you will be assigned chapter readings at the end of each session.

If you have not already obtained a copy of the book, you can purchase one at your local Christian supplier, order directly from the publisher by calling 800-852-8010, or order online at www.barbourbooks.com.

The purpose of this study is to deepen your understanding of the power, relevance, and reliability of God's Word. There is a certain mystery to God's book, and he wants you to discover its hidden treasures and the insights you need in order to deal with the challenges of life. Participating in this study with friends in a group will heighten that experience.

God wants you and your group to grasp the relevant truth in his Word that will transform, strengthen, and bring greater peace to your life. But more than that, God wants you to come to know him more deeply by studying his Word. "If you look for me wholeheartedly," God says, "you will find me. I will be found by you" (Jeremiah 29:13–14). This study is designed to give you greater confidence in God's Word and to motivate you to diligently seek—and find—its Author.

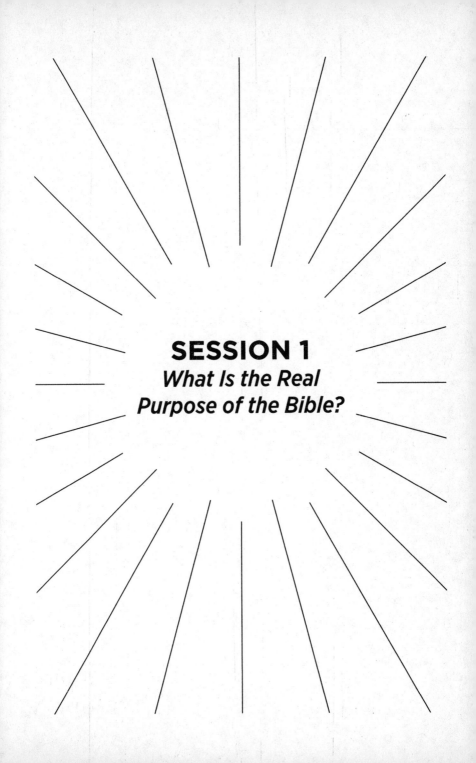

SESSION 1
What Is the Real Purpose of the Bible?

What Do You Think?

The Bible is an extraordinary book. In 2012 alone, the United Bible Societies distributed more than 400 million Bibles, Testaments, or smaller Scripture portions. The Bible is by far the most circulated book in all of history with billions in circulation.[1] It has now been translated into 2,650 languages, making it available in a familiar language to well over 90 percent of the world's population.

What is your earliest memory of seeing a Bible?

"I remember seeing a Bible when I was _____ years old. I recall reading the Bible on my own when I was _____ years old."

What is the Bible designed to do for us?

"I would say the Bible acts as a _____ and is designed to _____

_____

_____."

Session Objective

To discover the true purpose of God's Word and to strive to always read the Bible with God's core purpose in mind.

How Do You Respond?

Read 2 Timothy 3:16–17 aloud.

Based on these verses, what would you say the Bible is meant to accomplish in your life? In other words, what is its purpose?

_____

_____

_____

_____

Read Exodus 20:15–17 and Matthew 5:27–28 aloud.

What is the purpose of these types of commands and instructions?

_____

_____

_____

Read Romans 8:3 and 1 Corinthians 15:14 aloud.

What is the purpose of these types of verses? Why does the Bible give us this kind of information?

_____

_____

_____

Have someone in the group read aloud the following paragraphs, which are adapted from chapter 3 of *God-Breathed*.

Some people would say that God gave us his Word entirely for doctrinal and behavioral purposes. In other words, the Bible was written to teach us to think rightly and to live rightly. They might point to 2 Timothy to assert that correct beliefs and right living are what Scripture is all about: "All Scripture is inspired by God and profitable for teaching, for reproof, for correction" (2 Timothy 3:16 NASB).

Certainly doctrinal and behavioral guidance are part of God's purpose for Scripture. The English word teaching *in 2 Timothy 3:16 is from the Greek word* didaskalia, *which means "doctrine" or "correct thinking." So Paul is truly explaining that God gave us his Word so that we might believe correctly.*

The word correction *in this passage is from the Greek word* epanorthosis, *which means "restoration to an upright or right state of living" or "improvement in character." So Paul is certainly telling Timothy, and us, that the Bible is God's way of correcting us when we're wrong and restoring us to right living. Therefore, we have the Bible to teach us how to believe rightly and live rightly.*

Passages such as Romans 3:30 and 1 Corinthians 15:14 are there to teach us doctrinal truths—they help us think *rightly. Other passages, such as Exodus 20:15–17 and Matthew 5:27–28, are there to teach us behavioral truths—they help us* know *how to* live *rightly.*

Though this guidance is an important aspect of Scripture, it is not the full picture. The teachings of Scripture (doctrine) keep us thinking and believing rightly, and the instructions of Scripture (commands) keep us acting and living rightly. But without the proper context, we can miss the true purpose of Scripture, which is to guide us into keeping right thinking and right living in balance.

We can easily overemphasize the importance of the law and focus on knowing all the right doctrines. This can lead to arrogance and the acquisition of knowledge for the mere sake of having it. We can overemphasize adherence to the law, and this can lead to legalistic behavior and a judgmental attitude. Such legalism is what characterized the Pharisees in Jesus' day, who focused only on these two aspects of Scripture. Their believing and living were out of balance because they failed to understand the most important command of all.

Jesus explained the true purpose of Scripture when he answered a question posed to him by an expert in religious law.

Have someone in the group read aloud Matthew 22:36–40. Based on Jesus' answer, what is the purpose of Scripture in each of our lives?

_____

_____

_____

Have someone in the group read the following paragraph aloud:

> *Jesus told this Pharisee that the greatest, most important commandments are to love God with everything we have and to love our neighbors as we love ourselves. But Jesus didn't stop there. He followed up with a most profound statement: "The entire law and all the demands of the prophets are based on these two commandments" (Matthew 22:40). In other words, all right teaching and all right living hang on the commandments to love God and love one another. Jesus told this religious expert—and all of us—that Scripture was given to lead us into a deeper love relationship with the One who wrote the book, and then also with everyone around us.*

The Pharisees and other religious leaders had seemingly grasped the doctrinal and behavioral purposes of Scripture. But what they failed to understand was the connection between right *beliefs*, right *behavior*, and right *relationships*.

Do you see the connection? If so, describe in your own words how those three elements work together. In other words, what does it mean to say that the primary purpose of Scripture is a relational one?

_____

_____

_____

_____

_____

Read these verses aloud:

> *Moses begged God: "If you are pleased with me,*
> *teach me your ways so I may know you."*
> *(Exodus 33:13 NIV)*

> *Jesus prayed to his Father: "This is the way to have*
> *eternal life—to know you, the only true God, and*
> *Jesus Christ, the one you sent to earth." (John 17:3)*

> *God spoke through Hosea the prophet, who said:*
> *"Oh, that we might know the LORD! Let us press on*
> *to know him. . . . I want you to show love, not offer*
> *sacrifices. I want you to know me." (Hosea 6:3, 6)*

What is your response to the reality that the mighty God of
the universe is open enough to say, "I want you to know me"? Is
that hard for you to believe? Explain how that makes you feel.

_____

_____

_____

_____

_____

Have someone in the group read the following paragraphs aloud:

> *We may study God's Word for correct beliefs. We*
> *may even obey God's Word for right behavior. But*
> *we must not forget* why. *The relational God of the*
> *Bible wants us to* experience *his love and the love*
> *of those around us. God gave us the Bible because*

he wants an intimate loving relationship with us, wants us to enjoy intimate loving relationships with others, and wants our relationships together to extend into eternity.

The relational purpose of Scripture is a powerful reality—the amazing truth that God wants you to be in an intimate relationship with him. Take a moment to allow that truth to sink in. Think of Jesus, through his Holy Spirit, speaking directly to you in very intimate terms. He longs for you to know him intimately. He longs to fulfill you, complete you, and give you joy as you love him and love other people. That is why he has given you his Spirit and his Word. What does he say to you and me? Contemplate the words of Jesus below.

"You search the Scriptures because you think they give you eternal life. But the Scriptures point to me!" (John 5:39)

"My purpose is to give. . .a rich and satisfying life." (John 10:10)

"I have told you this so that my joy may be in you and that your joy may be complete. My command is this: Love each other as I have loved you." (John 15:11–12 NIV)

"I pray that they will all be one, just as you and I are one—as you are in me, Father, and I am in you. And may they be in us so that the world will believe you sent me." (John 17:21)

How might grasping more deeply the relational purpose of Scripture cause you to read the Bible differently?

How do you respond to the following statement? In the Bible God has written you a series of love letters, rather than a big instruction book intended simply to teach you how to think and live rightly.

_____

_____

_____

_____

_____

Apply It This Week

This week share with a friend or family member about the relational purpose of the Bible. Here are some conversation starters to help you:

- I've been studying lately about the purpose of the Bible. What would you say is the real purpose of the Bible?

- Our small group has been discussing the purpose of the Bible. I've been learning. . .

In a devotional time before God, read Psalm 145:13–21. Write a prayer of thanks to God for how he has been a relational God who has protected you and provided for you. Be specific about how God has protected you and provided for you.

_____

_____

_____

_____

_____

_____

This week, before the next group meeting, read chapters 1–4 in *God-Breathed*. Pay particular attention to what the book says about how the Bible is alive and powerful, as well as how it is to be interpreted. If you don't already have the *God-Breathed* book, you can obtain a copy from your local Christian supplier, order directly from the publisher by calling 800-852-8010, or order online at www.barbourbooks.com.

Close in Prayer

Pray that the truth you have encountered will become real, alive, and active in your life. Use this prayer time to express your desire to more deeply experience the power and relevance of God's Word.

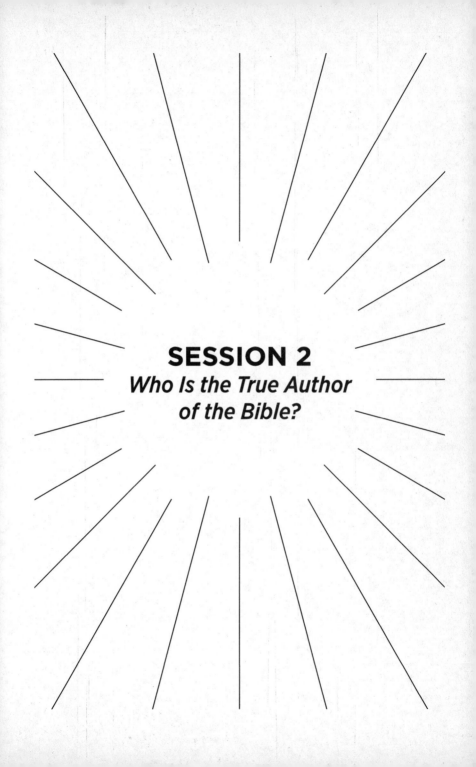

SESSION 2
Who Is the True Author of the Bible?

What Do You Think?

The apostle Paul writes that "all Scripture is inspired by God" (2 Timothy 3:16). The Bible contains sixty-six books—thirty-nine in the Old Testament and twenty-seven in the New Testament. These books were written between two thousand and three thousand years ago, through more than forty generations, by more than forty different writers from every walk of life. Think a moment about what Paul means when he says that all Scripture is inspired by God.

Have you ever been inspired by a song, a poem, or a speaker?

"The song _____ has inspired me. The poem _____ has been an inspiration to me. A speaker or person by the name of _____ has inspired me in the past."

A person, song, or poem may have inspired you and lifted your spirits, but is this the same kind of inspiration that Paul refers to when he says the Bible is inspired? What do you think Paul means when he writes that "Scripture is inspired by God"?

_____

_____

_____

_____

Session Objective

To determine who authored the Bible, identify what it means for the Bible to be inspired, and discover who decided which books would become Scripture.

How Do You Respond?

Exodus 31:18 says that the first set of tablets of the Ten Commandments was "written by the finger of God." Nowhere else do we find that God wrote his own words. All other Scripture was penned by men such as Moses, King David, the prophets, and the apostles of Jesus. If Scripture is God's Word, what did God do—put these people into some kind of trance in order to take control of their hands and pens to write out his message to us? And if he didn't do that, how can Scripture be considered the "Word of God"? Discuss these questions as a group.

_____

_____

_____

_____

_____

_____

Have someone in the group read aloud the following paragraphs, which are adapted from chapter 6 of *God-Breathed*.

> *The word* inspired *is translated from the Greek word* theopneustos, *which literally means "God-breathed" (*theos, *God;* pneō, *to breathe). In other words, God breathed out his words to men, who in turn wrote them down. These men were not God's mindless dictation machines, nor were they placed in a hypnotic state to transmit God's words in writing. Rather, God revealed to their minds what he wanted them to write, and they, as his willing servants, put into writing what he wanted them*

to say. These men used their own writing skills and talents, but they were very cognizant that the thoughts and words they were writing came directly from God.

The apostle Peter sums it up like this: "No prophecy in Scripture ever came from the prophet's own understanding, or from human initiative. No, those prophets were moved by the Holy Spirit, and they spoke from God" (2 Peter 1:20–21). Peter says that the Holy Spirit superintended God's words so that men wrote what he wanted them to write. Men were God's instruments to convey his message. The apostle Paul makes the same point when he writes, "When we tell you these things, we do not use words that come from human wisdom. Instead, we speak words given to us by the Spirit, using the Spirit's words to explain spiritual truths" (1 Corinthians 2:13).

Paul reemphasized this truth to the church in Galatia when he wrote, "I want you to understand that the gospel message I preach is not based on mere human reasoning. I received my message from no human source, and no one taught me. Instead, I received it by direct revelation from Jesus Christ" (Galatians 1:11–12).

Practically every person through whom God chose to inscribe his message made it clear that God was the source of that message. That's why we say that God is the author of Scripture and men were his writers. It was God's spiritual truths conveyed

through men to the written page. So when we read
the writings of Moses, David, Solomon, Isaiah,
Jeremiah, Matthew, Mark, Luke, John, Peter,
Paul, and all the other spokesmen of God, we can be
assured that we are reading God's words.

Some people say the Bible has supernatural power. Why do you think some believe that is true? Read Hebrews 4:12–13 aloud and discuss together as a group.

_____

_____

_____

_____

Have someone in the group read the following paragraphs aloud:

The Scriptures are alive and have supernatural
power because they are from a living God who is
here today in the person of the Holy Spirit.

But wait a minute. There may be sixty-six
books we call the Bible, but how do we know that
these particular books are the ones God inspired?

On a scale of 1 to 10 (10 being the highest), how confident are you that the sixty-six books of the Bible are the only books that are inspired Scripture? _____

Were the people who decided which books would be considered Scripture infallible? Could they have overlooked some God-breathed writings or included some that were not God's inspired words? What do you think? Discuss together as a group.

_____

_____

_____

_____

_____

_____

Suppose you lived centuries ago and God chose you as one of his inspired writers. How do you think you would know that God was speaking through you?

_____

_____

_____

_____

How did Moses know that God was speaking through him? (Read Exodus 33:11.)

_____

_____

_____

_____

How did Isaiah the prophet know that God was speaking through him? (Read Isaiah 1:1.)

_____

_____

How did the prophet Joel know that God was speaking through him? (Read Joel 1:1.)

_____

_____

Have someone in the group read the following paragraphs aloud:

> *God chose numerous ways and means to convey his words through his spokesmen. Moses told the children of Israel that "the LORD your God will raise up for you a prophet like me. . . . The LORD said to me, '. . .I will put my words in his mouth, and he will tell the people everything I command him'" (Deuteronomy 18:15, 17–18).*
>
> *Sometimes God communicated to his spokesmen through dreams, as he did with Joseph in Genesis 37. In the case of Isaiah, Ezekiel, Daniel, the apostle John, and others, God spoke to them through visions. At other times, God sent angels to visit his writers (Genesis 19). But most often, the words came through an inner voice of God's Spirit represented in the phrase "according to the word of the Lord." This choice of words is used more than three thousand*

times throughout Scripture. God wanted us to know him and how we could have a relationship with him, so he carefully communicated "the words of the Lord" through his human spokesmen.

The thirty-nine books of the Old Testament were officially recognized as God-inspired Scripture as early as the fourth century BC and certainly no later than 150 BC. These books were originally grouped into three major divisions: five books of the Law of Moses, eight books of the Prophets, and eleven books under the umbrella designation of Writings.

The Jewish priests and people recognized these thirty-nine books as God-inspired. A certain person who recognized the Old Testament was truly God's Word would give us even greater assurance. Who might that person be?

_____

_____

Have someone in the group read aloud the following paragraphs, which are adapted from chapter 7 of *God-Breathed*.

The most definitive recognition that the whole of the Old Testament was God-breathed came from none other than Jesus himself. He not only quoted and repeatedly taught from the Old Testament, but he specifically referred to its three sections when he said, "Everything written about me in the law of Moses [the five books] and the prophets [the eight books] and in the Psalms [included in the eleven writings] must be fulfilled" (Luke 24:44).

*Jesus also cited the entire span of the Hebrew
text (our Old Testament), from its first book to its
last, when he referred to the first and last martyrs
within its pages. He said, "This generation will be
held responsible for the murder of all God's prophets
from the creation of the world—from the murder
of Abel to the murder of Zechariah" (Luke 11:50–
51). This was the same as saying "from Genesis to
Malachi." This quote from Luke 11 clearly confirms
that Jesus accepted the entire Old Testament canon.*

How about the New Testament? All twenty-seven books of
the New Testament were written approximately forty years
after Jesus ascended into heaven, and certainly no later than
AD 100. What do you think made the early church realize that
those writings were God-inspired? Discuss together as a group.

_____

_____

_____

_____

_____

Have someone in the group read the following paragraphs
aloud:

*During the middle of the first century AD, small
churches sprang up throughout the known world
as a result of the apostles' writings. The people
receiving these writings knew they had come from*

men who had known Jesus personally or were considered authorities on him and his teaching. Therefore they recognized that the documents being circulated were God's inspired words empowered by the very presence of the Holy Spirit.

Though some divisions occurred among the churches during this time, there was an amazing unity and focus of purpose and teaching. This was because every group appealed to apostolic authority. It was the writings of the apostles, or men close to and endorsed by them, that each group believed were supernaturally guided by God to reveal the teachings and truth about Jesus Christ.

You may have heard that an ancient church council, such as the council of Hippo (AD 393) and the council of Carthage (AD 397), decided which books of the Bible, namely the New Testament, were considered Scripture. But actually no one person, organization, or group determined which letters or writings of the apostles were to be granted the status of Scripture. Rather, individuals, and most notably the early church throughout the known world, recognized or discovered which books were God-breathed from their very inception. In other words, no group gave a particular writing the authority of being Scripture; the writings themselves, through the power of the Holy Spirit, made it clear that God had divinely appointed them as Scripture.

There was, however, a standard or rule
established to guide the early church in its discovery
of which writings were authentic, God-inspired
Scripture. The discovery process led to the inclusion
of a certain group of books that are referred to as
the canon *of Scripture.* Canon *comes from the*
Greek word kanōn, *meaning "measuring rod" or*
"rule." From biblical and church history, we find
at least four measurements or rules that guided the
church leaders in recognizing which writings were
divinely inspired:

1. The writing was authored by an apostle or prophet of God or by someone closely connected with one or more of the apostles or prophets.
2. The writings clearly evidenced the confirming power and presence of God.
3. The message was consistent with other recognized Scripture.
4. The writing was widely accepted by the church from an early date.

Have you heard about other spiritual writings that some claim are equal to the sixty-six books of Scripture? Share what you know about these writings.

_____

_____

_____

_____

Do you believe these other writings are God-inspired? Why or why not?

_____

_____

_____

_____

_____

_____

Have someone in the group read the following paragraphs aloud:

Fourteen books emerged as spiritual writings that some thought should be included as Scripture in the Old Testament. Now called the Apocrypha, these added books surfaced between 200 BC and the early second century AD. They include

- First Esdras
- Second Esdras
- Tobit
- Judith
- Additions to Esther
- The Wisdom of Solomon
- Ecclesiasticus
- Baruch
- Susanna
- Bel and the Dragon (additions to Daniel)
- The Song of the Three Hebrew Children (additions to Daniel)

- The Prayer of Manasseh
- First Maccabees
- Second Maccabees

Some people believe these fourteen books should be added to the twenty-four canonized books of the Hebrew text, and some have added them to the Greek Septuagint translation of the Old Testament. The Jewish leaders, however, recognized only the original twenty-four books of the Hebrew text as Scripture—the same books Jesus had confirmed. Also, it can be noted that Jesus never quoted from any of the added fourteen books. He cited only from the twenty-four books recognized as the Jewish canon—the same reordered thirty-nine books we have today. Luke 24:27 uses the phrase "all the Scriptures" when referring to the Old Testament, which confirms that Jesus accepted the same complete Hebrew books that Judaism recognized as canonical at the time.

Today these fourteen books are still in existence and are referred to as the Apocrypha, which means "that which is hidden." Though these books were not accepted by the early church or the Jewish scholars as late as 150 BC, they were eventually included in the Old Testament by the Roman Catholic Church in AD 1546.

The Protestant Bible does not include the Apocrypha in the Old Testament for the reasons cited above. Protestant scholars also point out that none of the fourteen books of the Apocrypha claims divine inspiration. In fact, some actually disclaim inspiration. They also explain that highly respected Jewish philosophers such as Philo Judaeus of Alexandria, historians such as Josephus, and translators such as the renowned Jerome, as well as the early church fathers, rejected the Apocrypha as God-breathed Scripture.

Though the twenty-seven books of the New Testament were unofficially recognized as Scripture by the church as early as AD 100, some wondered whether certain other spiritual writings were also God-breathed. By the middle of the second century, a number of writings emerged, known as the New Testament Apocrypha and Gnostic writings. These include the Infancy Gospel of Thomas, the Gospel of Thomas, the Gospel of Peter, and the Gospel of Judas.

These writings by and large contradict the Gospels of Matthew, Mark, Luke, and John and Paul's epistles. Some of their contradictory teachings include the idea that there were multiple creators; that salvation is by "spiritual knowledge"; that ignorance, not sin, is humanity's problem; and other teachings that were refuted in the twenty-seven books of the New Testament. The Infancy Gospel of Thomas, a Gnostic writing, depicts a scene in which a young Jesus reacts to being bumped into by some children by striking them down with his supernatural power.

All of these added spiritual writings were rejected by the early church and were, in part, why *the church fathers established a set of rules in the first place for recognizing which writings were truly inspired by God.*

Do you understand why the early church established rules by which to recognize which writings were God-breathed? Review the four rules of the canon. To what degree do you feel confident that, in the sixty-six books of the Bible, we have all the God-inspired writings God wants us to have? Discuss together as a group.

_____

_____

_____

_____

_____

Apply It This Week

This week, share with a friend or family member how the Bible is God's inspired Word. Here are some conversation starters to help you:

- Many people believe the Bible is God's inspired Word. Do you believe that? Why or why not?
- I have been studying why we consider the Bible to be God's inspired Word. I've been learning. . .

In a devotional time before God, read Psalm 19:7–11. Write out the words the psalmist uses to describe the laws and commands of God's Word. Write a heartfelt prayer of thanks for what God's Word means to you.

_____

_____

_____

_____

_____

_____

This week, before the next group meeting, read chapters 5–8 in _God-Breathed._ These chapters will solidify and expand on what you have learned in this session.

Close in Prayer
Pray that the truth you have encountered will become real, alive, and active in your life. Use this prayer time to express your desire to more deeply experience the power and relevance of God's Word.

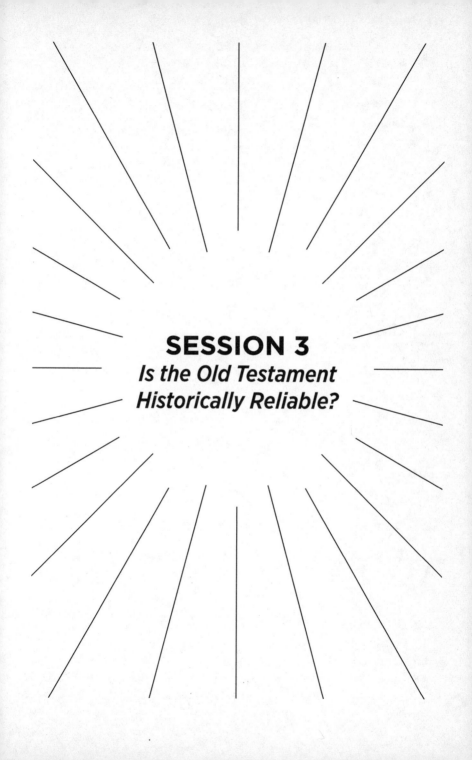

SESSION 3
*Is the Old Testament
Historically Reliable?*

What Do You Think?

Have you ever heard someone tell a true story, but you sensed that he or she exaggerated or embellished a bit? Share the story and what was exaggerated. (Avoid sharing the person's name, to protect the guilty.)

_____

_____

_____

_____

Have someone in the group read the following paragraphs aloud:

> *Moses penned the first five books of the Bible more than three thousand years ago. The other books of the Old Testament were completed by around 460 BC. All the New Testament books were written perhaps as early as AD 70, and no later than AD 100. The Bible was not printed until the mid-1400s. So anything that was written prior to that time had to be recopied by scribes if it was going to be preserved for future generations.*
>
> *None of the original manuscripts of Scripture have been found. Every manuscript that exists today is a copy of a copy of a copy. So how do we know that God didn't give Moses only seven commandments, and some scribe along the way decided to add three more? How do we know that a weary copier, bleary-eyed from lack of sleep, didn't skip a few critical words of Jesus, leave out*

entire sections of the book of John, or embellish the
messages from Paul's letters?

Does it really matter if we don't have accurate copies of what was originally written by those who were inspired by God? What difference does it make if there were only seven commandments and scribes added three more to make ten? What problem, if any, do you see with having inaccurate copies of Scripture?

_____

_____

_____

_____

Have someone in the group read the following paragraph aloud:

> *If the original words that God gave to Moses*
> *or the prophets were later changed or carelessly*
> *copied, how could we be sure we were getting the*
> *words that God intended? The Bible, in part, is a*
> *revelation of the character and nature of God. If we*
> *possess a distorted revelation, we have—at best—*
> *an incomplete picture of what God is like. Without*
> *a reliable Bible, we have no assurance that the*
> *truths we follow and obey are true at all.*

Session Objective
To gain a greater understanding of how and why we can trust the Old Testament to be a reliable revelation of God.

How Do You Respond?

Since we don't have the original writings of the Old Testament, how can we know that the copies we do have are reliable? How can we know whether any ancient writing is reliable? Do you know of any test to measure the reliability of the copies of historical records?

_____

_____

_____

_____

Have someone in the group read aloud the following paragraphs, which are adapted from chapters 9–11 of *God-Breathed*.

There are three basic principles or tests to determine the reliability of an ancient historical record.

- *The Bibliographical Test*
  To evaluate the reliability of an ancient writing, we ask two fundamental questions:

  1. *How many manuscript copies of that document have survived?*
  2. *What interval of time elapsed between the original writing and the earliest existing copy?*

This bibliographical test assesses the trustworthiness of any work of literature based on the wise supposition that the more copies we can gather of a work—and the nearer in time those copies are to the original—the greater our certainty that we possess the text as originally written. The more copies we have of an original writing, the better we can compare one to another to see if they are consistent. Ideally, they will be close replicas of each other. And it stands to reason that the earliest copy made from the original would be the most trustworthy. The more removed a copy is from the original, the greater the chances that any copying mistakes would be replicated in subsequent copies.

- The External Evidence Test
  This test helps scholars evaluate an ancient writing's reliability by examining evidence outside the writing itself. This test determines whether other historical materials confirm or conflict with the internal testimony of the document itself. In other words, can writings be found apart from the literature under analysis that substantiate its accuracy, reliability, and authenticity?

- The Internal Evidence Test
  This third test weighs whether a book is consistent within itself and whether the authors can be trusted to tell the truth. Is the book filled with errors and contradictions? Is there evidence that the bias of the writers caused them to lose objectivity and distort the facts?

We will look more closely at the external and internal evidence tests for the New Testament in the next session. First, let's put the Old Testament to the bibliographical test and examine other ancient pieces of literature to make a comparison. Fill in the chart based on the historical information about the various ancient writings covered in this session.

A COMPARISON OF ANCIENT WORKS WITH THE OLD TESTAMENT

Author	Work	Date Written By or Between	Earliest MSS	Time Gap in Years	# of MSS
Plato	Tetralogies				
Caesar	*Gallic Wars*				
Homer	*Iliad*				
	Old Testament from Moses & other OT writers	_____ _____	_____ _____	_____ _____	

Have someone in the group read the following paragraphs aloud:

- The philosopher Plato, a student of Socrates, lived some four centuries before Christ. Plato was a prolific author. His Tetralogies were written in 400 BC. [Fill in the "Date Written By or Between" on the chart above.] The earliest manuscript of Plato's Tetralogies in existence today is dated to AD 895 and is housed in the Bodleian Library at the University of Oxford. There are 210 manuscripts of Plato's Tetralogies surviving today. [Fill in the "Earliest MSS" and "# of MSS" on the chart.]

- What is the time gap between Plato's original writing and the earliest manuscript dated at AD 895? _____. [Fill in the "Time Gap in Years" on the chart.]

- Julius Caesar wrote about the Gallic Wars, which lasted from 58 BC to 50 BC. The last book of *Gallic Wars* was composed no later than 44 BC. [Fill in the "Date Written By or Between" on the chart above.]

  There are 250+ manuscripts of Caesar's *Gallic Wars* in existence today. The earliest one is dated to AD 900. What is the time gap between the writing of *Gallic Wars* and the earliest manuscript copy in existence? _____ [Fill in the "Time Gap in Years," the "Earliest MSS," and "# of MSS" on the chart.]

- Homer's *Iliad*, a highly recognized ancient writing, was penned in 800 BC. [Fill in the "Date Written By or Between" on the chart above.]

  More than 1,800 *Iliad* manuscripts have survived, and the earliest copy is dated to circa 400 BC. [Fill in the "Earliest MSS" and "# of MSS" on the chart.]

  What is the time gap between the writing of the *Iliad* and the earliest surviving manuscript? _____ [Fill in the "Time Gap in Years" on the chart.]

These three samples of ancient literature are considered highly reliable according to the bibliographical test. To have somewhere between 200 and more than 1,800 existing manuscripts is a very respectable number. And a time interval between 400 and 1,300 years between the original and the earliest existing copy is impressive. No scholar today would question the reliability of these works based on this first test.

So how do you think the Old Testament manuscripts would stand up to this test? Make an estimate of how many Old Testament scrolls and manuscripts are in existence today. Share your estimate with the group.

_____

_____

Have someone in the group read aloud the following paragraphs, which are adapted from chapter 11 of *God-Breathed*.

> *In the late nineteenth century, almost 250,000 Jewish manuscript fragments of the Old Testament were found in the* genizah *(a storeroom or cabinet for old manuscripts) of the Ben Ezra Synagogue in Old Cairo. Those documents were written from about AD 870 to AD 1880.[2] A few years ago, more than 24,000 biblical-related materials were published from this Cairo Genizah Collection.*

> *A medieval bound Hebrew manuscript called the Aleppo Codex was copied in about AD 925.* Codex *is the term used for a book made up of sheets of leather (parchment or vellum) rather than linked in scroll form. Many scholars consider the*

Aleppo Codex to be the most authoritative copy of the Masoretic text. Originally copied as a complete Hebrew text (Old Testament), only 294 of the original 487 manuscript pages survive today.

The Leningrad Codex (AD 1008), a complete copy of the entire Hebrew text, is housed in the National Library of Russia. Practically all modern English translations of the Old Testament are based on the Leningrad Codex.

Assuming Moses wrote the first five books of the Old Testament in the later years of his life, he would have penned them around 1350 BC. What would be the time interval between Moses' writings and the earliest known manuscript as mentioned above?

_____

_____

_____

Is the time gap between the original writings of Moses and the earliest known copies a concern to you? Discuss with the group.

_____

_____

_____

_____

_____

_____

Have someone in the group read the following paragraphs aloud:

Even though the elapsed time between the original writing of the Old Testament and the date of the earliest manuscripts in existence today is not optimal, one has to take into consideration just how carefully these writings were copied through the ages.

One of the ways God ensured his Word would be relayed accurately was by choosing, calling, and cultivating a nation of men and women who took the Hebrew text very seriously. A reverent attitude toward the commands of God became such a part of the Jewish identity that a class of Jewish scholars, called the Sopherim, *from a Hebrew word meaning "scribes," arose between the fifth and third centuries BC. These custodians of the Hebrew Scriptures dedicated themselves to carefully preserving the ancient manuscripts and producing new copies when necessary.*

The Sopherim, who initiated a stringent standard of meticulous discipline, were subsequently eclipsed by the Talmudic scribes, who guarded, interpreted, and commented on the sacred texts from AD 100 to AD 500. In turn, the Talmudic scribes were followed by the better-known and even more meticulous Masoretic scribes (AD 500–900).

The Talmudic scribes established detailed and stringent disciplines for copying a manuscript. Their rules were so rigorous that when a new copy was complete, they gave the reproduction equal authority to that of its parent because they were thoroughly convinced that they had an exact duplicate.

The Talmudic guidelines for copying manuscripts included the following:

- The scroll must be made of the skin of a ceremonially clean animal.
- Each skin must contain a specified number of columns, equal throughout the entire book.
- The length of each column must extend no less than forty-eight lines or more than sixty lines.
- The column breadth must consist of exactly thirty letters.
- The space of a thread must appear between every consonant.
- The breadth of nine consonants must be inserted between each section.
- A space of three lines must appear between each book.
- The fifth book of Moses (Deuteronomy) must conclude exactly with a full line.
- Nothing—not even the shortest word— could be copied from memory; everything had to be copied letter by letter.
- The scribe must count the number of times each letter of the alphabet occurred in each book and compare it to the original.

God instilled in these scribes such a painstaking reverence for the Hebrew Scriptures to ensure the amazingly accurate transmission of his Word.

Discuss together how the discipline of the Hebrew scribes in copying the Scriptures increases your confidence in the reliability of the Old Testament.

_____

_____

_____

_____

_____

_____

Have someone in the group read the following paragraphs aloud:

Until recently, we had no way of knowing just how amazing the preservation of the Old Testament is. Then, in the spring of 1947, a young Bedouin shepherd made the greatest manuscript discovery of all time.

On the west side of the Dead Sea, about eight miles south of Jericho near an ancient site called Qumran, this young shepherd discovered a cave containing several large jars that held leather scrolls wrapped in linen cloth.

Once archaeologists completed their search of the Qumran caves—eleven caves in all— almost 1,050 scrolls had been found in about

25,000 to 50,000 pieces (a number that varies depending on how the fragments are counted).[3] Of these manuscripts, about three hundred were texts from the Bible, and many of the rest had "direct relevance to early Judaism and emerging Christianity."[4] Every book of the Old Testament was represented, except for the book of Esther, and the earliest copies dated from about 250 BC.

With the discovery of the Dead Sea Scrolls, as the Qumran manuscripts are commonly known, we now have Old Testament texts 1,175 years older than the very reliable Aleppo Codex. We can also compare the Leningrad Codex to the Dead Sea Scrolls, which are 1,258 years older.

Now here's the exciting part: Once the Dead Sea Scrolls were translated and compared with modern versions of the Hebrew Bible, the text proved to be identical, word for word, in more than 95 percent of the cases. (The 5 percent deviation consists mainly of spelling variations. For example, of the 166 words in Isaiah 53, only seventeen letters are in question. Of those, ten are a matter of spelling, and four are stylistic differences; the remaining three letters comprise the word light, which was added to Isaiah 53:11.)

In other words, the greatest manuscript discovery of all time revealed that more than one thousand years of copying the Old Testament had produced only very minor variations, none of which altered the clear meaning of the text or brought the manuscript's fundamental integrity into question.

With the new information above, what is the time gap between Moses' first writings (around 1350 BC) and the earliest Dead Sea Scroll copies (250 BC)?

_____

_____

The other thirty-four books of the Old Testament were written later, some as late as 460 BC. What is the time gap between these later books and the earliest Dead Sea Scroll copies, which are dated to 250 BC?

_____

_____

Now fill in the comparison chart with your information of "Date Written By or Between," "Earliest MSS," and "Time Gap in Years." You will need to fill in two sets of numbers, one for Moses' writings and the other for the rest of the Old Testament.

When we add up all the Hebrew texts from hand-copied scrolls and manuscripts in existence today that are dated earlier than the eighteenth century AD, we come to an estimate of at least 17,000 Old Testament scrolls and manuscripts. [Add that number to your chart under "# of MSS."]

How do your new figures compare to those for the other reliable works of ancient literature? Do these figures provide you an even greater confidence in the reliability of the Old Testament? Share your thoughts with the group.

_____

_____

_____

_____

_____

_____

Apply It This Week

This week, share with a friend or family member about the reliability of the Old Testament. Here are some conversation starters to help you:

- Some people have said you can't trust the Old Testament because we don't have the original writings of Moses and the prophets. Has that concerned you? Why or why not?

- I have been studying how reliable the Old Testament is in my small group. I've discovered. . .

In a devotional time before God, read Psalm 19:30–35. Write a prayer expressing your desire to follow God's reliable Word and thank him that he has revealed himself to you as a God who loves you dearly.

_____

_____

_____

_____

_____

_____

This week, before the next group meeting, read chapters 9–11 in *God-Breathed*. These chapters will provide greater insight into the reliability of the Old Testament.

Close in Prayer

Pray that the truth you have encountered will become real, alive, and active in your life. Use this prayer time to express your desire to more deeply experience the power and relevance of God's Word.

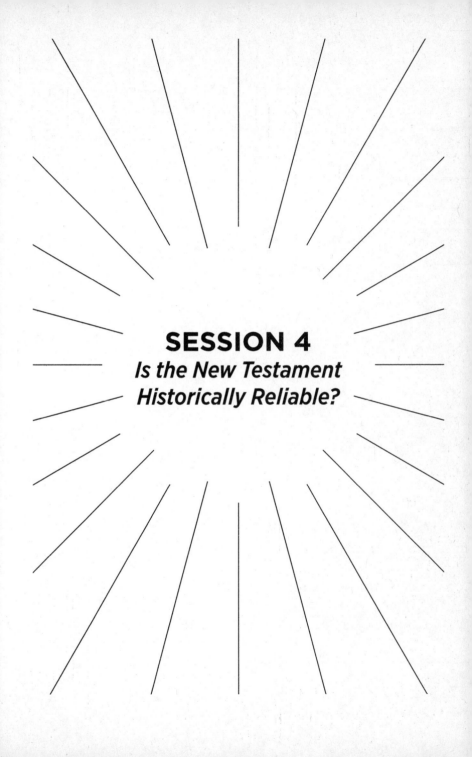

SESSION 4
Is the New Testament Historically Reliable?

What Do You Think?

The New Testament writers, specifically the writers of the Gospels, reported on what Jesus said and the events surrounding his life and death. How important is it to know that what the apostles wrote has been accurately preserved and handed down? What difference would it make to you if you found out that the words Jesus spoke had been changed or that details about his death or reports about his resurrection were altered in the copying process? Discuss your answers with the group.

_____

_____

_____

_____

Session Objective

To obtain a greater understanding of how and why we can trust the New Testament's reliability, as well as to develop greater confidence in the Old Testament when put to the external evidence test.

How Do You Respond?

Let's put the New Testament to the bibliographical test and examine two other ancient pieces of literature alongside it for comparison. Fill in the chart based on the historical information about the ancient writings covered in this section.

A COMPARISON OF ANCIENT WORKS
WITH THE NEW TESTAMENT

Author	Work	Date Written By or Between	Earliest MSS	Time Gap in Years	# of MSS
Livy	*History of Rome*				
Pliny, the Elder	*Natural History*				
	New Testament				
	Greek NT, early translations				

Have someone in the group read aloud the following paragraphs, which are adapted from chapter 12 of *God-Breathed*.

- Titus Livius Patavinus—commonly known as Livy—was a famous Roman historian who wrote the *History of Rome* between 59 BC and AD 17. [Fill in the "Date Written By or Between" on the chart above.]

  There are ninety known copies of Livy's *History of Rome* in existence, and the earliest manuscript copy is dated to the early fifth century (circa AD 400). [Fill in the "Earliest MSS" and "# of MSS" on the chart.]

  What is the average time gap between Livy's original writing and the earliest manuscript, dated to AD 400?
  _____ [Fill in the "Time Gap in Years" on the chart.]

- Pliny the Elder, a Roman author and natural philosopher, wrote his *Natural History* between AD 49 and AD 79. [Fill in the "Date Written By or Between" on the chart.]

There are two hundred copies of Pliny's work in existence today, with one manuscript fragment dated to the fifth century, and the others to the fourteenth or fifteenth century. [Fill in "# of MSS" and two dates under "Earliest MSS" on the chart.]

What is the average time gap between Pliny's original writings and the earliest surviving manuscripts? _____ [Fill in the "Time Gap in Years" on the chart.]

- The books of the New Testament were written as early as AD 50 and no later than AD 100. There are more than 5,830 manuscripts in existence, and a fragment of the Gospel of John, located in the John Rylands Library in Manchester, England, has been dated to within fifty years of when John penned the original. The others are dated to AD 130. [Fill in the "Date Written By or Between," "Earliest MSS," "# of MSS," and "Time Gap in Years" on the chart.]

In addition, more than 18,000 Greek New Testament translations exist, with the earliest manuscripts dated between AD 400 and AD 500. [Fill in the "Date Written By or Between," "Earliest MSS," "# of MSS," and "Time Gap in Years" on the chart.]

How does the New Testament rank in comparison to the other two highly reliable first-century pieces of literature when measured by the bibliographical test? What do you think accounts for so many ancient New Testament manuscripts in existence today?

_____

_____

_____

_____

The External Evidence Test

Have someone in the group read the following paragraph aloud:

> *The external evidence test examines writings apart from Scripture that can substantiate its reliability. The authenticity of the biblical record has been bolstered because key people near the time when the original New Testament writings were penned actually quoted these writings.*

Take an educated (or uneducated) guess of how many New Testament quotes can be documented prior to AD 325. Of these, how many New Testament books do you think have been quoted?

_____

_____

_____

Have someone in the group read the following paragraph aloud:

> *The apostles' writings were so esteemed and widely distributed that the early church fathers quoted from them extensively. In fact, their quotations*

are so extensive that the New Testament could virtually be reconstructed from them without use of New Testament manuscripts.[5]

The chart below documents more than 36,000 citations by just seven early Christian leaders prior to AD 325.

EARLY CITATIONS OF THE NEW TESTAMENT

Writer	Gospels	Acts	Pauline Epistles	General Epistles	Revelation	Totals
Justin Martyr	268	10	43	6	3	330
Irenaeus	1,038	194	499	23	65	1,819
Clement of Alexandria	1,017	44	1,127	207	11	2,406
Origen	9,231	349	7,778	399	165	17,922
Tertullian	3,822	502	2,609	120	205	7,258
Hippolytus	734	42	387	27	188	1,378
Eusebius	3,258	211	1,592	88	27	5,176
Grand Totals	**19,368**	**1,352**	**14,035**	**870**	**664**	**36,289**

Read Hebrews 4:12 and 2 Timothy 3:16–17 aloud. Why do you think the apostles' writings were quoted so often?

_____

_____

_____

_____

Have someone in the group read the following paragraphs aloud:

Apart from leading Christians in the early church who quoted the apostles, other non-Christian historians during the first century also verified the apostles' writings. Here is a sample of just three, from among scores of writers who confirmed the people, places, and events recorded in the New Testament.

- **Tacitus,** *a first-century Roman, is considered one of the most accurate historians of the ancient world. He mentions Pontius Pilatus and refers to the claim of Jesus' resurrection.*

- **Suetonius** *was chief secretary to Emperor Hadrian, who reigned in Rome from AD 117 to AD 138. He confirms the report in Acts 18:2 that Claudius commanded all Jews to leave Rome in AD 49.[6]*

- *Then there is* **Josephus,** *the famous Jewish historian (AD 37–AD 100). His writings contain many statements that verify the historical nature of both the Old and New Testaments. For example, Josephus refers to Jesus as the brother of James who was martyred. He writes that Ananias the high priest "assembled the Sanhedrin of the judges, and brought before them the brother of Jesus, who was called Christ, whose name was James, and some others, and when he had formed an accusation against them as breakers of the law, he delivered them to be stoned."[7] This passage, written in AD 93, confirms, within the first century, the New Testament reports that Jesus was a real person, that he was*

identified by others as the Christ, and that
he had a brother named James who died
a martyr's death at the hands of the high
priest and the Sanhedrin.

These and many other outside sources give far more
substantiation of the reliability of the biblical
record than can be found for any other book in
ancient history.

With such bibliographical and external evidence that the New
Testament is a reliable historical account, it would be illogical
to doubt that it is from God. So why do some people still
consider Jesus a mythical figure and doubt that he has provided
for our eternal salvation?

_____

_____

_____

_____

The Internal Evidence Test

Have someone in the group read the following paragraphs aloud:

The internal evidence test evaluates whether an
author can be trusted to tell the truth. It asks two
key questions: (1) Is the book filled with errors
and contradictions? and (2) Did the authors
distort the facts?

One way to determine whether authors can be
trusted is to examine the source material they draw
from to make their reports.

Read Luke 1:1–2 aloud. Where did the writers of the New Testament get their information?

_____

_____

Where did Luke get his information to write the Gospel of Luke?

_____

_____

Read John 19:35 aloud. Where did the report of Christ's death come from that John writes about?

_____

_____

Read 1 John 1:5 aloud. Where did John hear the message he reported on?

_____

_____

Read 2 Peter 1:16 aloud. Where did Peter get the stories he wrote about?

_____

_____

Read Luke 1:3–4 aloud. What does Luke say about his writing process that engenders trust in his account?

_____

_____

Have someone in the group read aloud the following paragraphs, which are adapted from chapter 13 of *God-Breathed*.

Some people think it would have been easy for Jesus' disciples to make up the many stories about Jesus. Not true. These eyewitnesses are considered extremely credible because they appealed to the knowledge of their readers—even their harshest opponents—who easily could have contradicted any false accounts. Yet these writers of Scripture invited correction by eyewitnesses to their claims when they said such things as the following:

- *"People of Israel, listen! God publicly endorsed Jesus the Nazarene by doing powerful miracles, wonders, and signs through him, as* you well know.*" (Acts 2:22, emphasis added)*

- *At this point Festus interrupted Paul's defense. "You are out of your mind, Paul!" he shouted. "Your great learning is driving you insane." "I am not insane, most excellent Festus," Paul replied. "What I am saying is true and reasonable. The king is familiar with these things, and I can speak freely to him. I am convinced that* none of this has escaped his notice, because it was not done in a corner.*" (Acts 26:24–26 NIV, emphasis added)*

We find similar appeals in Acts 2:32; 3:15; 13:31; and 1 Corinthians 15:3–8.

The disciples, in effect, were saying, "Check it out, ask around; you know this as well as we do!" Such challenges demonstrate a supreme confidence that what they recorded was not fabricated in any way. The disciples spoke directly to those who violently opposed them, saying, "You, too, know these facts are true. We dare you to disprove us!" That, of course, would be a foolish approach if they were spreading lies.

According to Scripture and tradition, the majority of the original disciples died as martyrs for their faith in Christ. How many people would be willing to die for a lie? How does that fact further reinforce the belief that the apostles wrote the truth about Jesus and believed in him themselves? Discuss your answer with the group.

_____

_____

_____

_____

What about Moses?

Have someone in the group read the following paragraph aloud:

No other writer of Scripture has been more under question by the critics than Moses. Jewish and conservative Christian scholars have long recognized that Moses wrote the first five books of the Old Testament (the Pentateuch). The dates of his writings are believed to be during the Bronze Age (1500s BC–1200s BC). But the critics contend that the Pentateuch is a collection of writings from numerous sources, by different groups of people, who gathered the information between 850 BC and 445 BC. According to this notion, the books previously ascribed to Moses were actually collected over time and not compiled until sometime around 400 BC. This would, of course, preclude Moses from being the writer because it is almost a thousand years after his death in approximately 1350 BC. The main reason critics assert that Moses did not write the Pentateuch is their claim that writing had not yet been invented when Moses lived.

Read Exodus 33:11 aloud. Does it really matter whether Moses was the writer of the Pentateuch? Why or why not? Where did Moses supposedly get his information about the Creation story, the fall of Adam and Eve, the Flood, etc?

_____

_____

_____

_____

Have someone in the group read the following evidence aloud that disputes the critics' claims that Moses is not the author of the Pentateuch.

In 1976 an Italian archaeologist named Paolo Matthiae discovered what became known as the Ebla Tablets—more than 16,000 clay tablets dating from 2400 BC. This discovery delivered a crushing blow to the supposition that writing was nonexistent in the days of Moses and thus he could not have written the Pentateuch. The critics claimed that the period described in the Mosaic narrative (1400 BC) was prior to all knowledge of writing. But the Ebla findings demonstrate that one thousand years before Moses, there were laws, customs, and events recorded in writing from the same area of the world in which Moses lived.

Historical critics contended not only that the time of Moses was prior to the invention of writing, but also that the priestly code and legislation recorded in the Pentateuch are too far advanced to have been written by Moses. They alleged that the Israelites at that time were too primitive to have developed anything of such high sophistication, and that it wasn't until about the first half of the Persian period (538 BC–331 BC) that such detailed legislation was recorded.

However, the Ebla tablets containing the law codes demonstrate that elaborate judicial proceedings and case law were in existence centuries before Moses. Many are very similar to the Deuteronomic law code (e.g., Deuteronomy 22:22–30) to which critics have persistently attributed a very late date.

More recent archaeological finds also give credibility to Moses' writings. These discoveries contradict the assumption that the Pentateuch was written hundreds of years after Moses. For example, in 1986, archaeologists in Jerusalem discovered a *biblical text older than the Dead Sea Scrolls. Part of the text of Numbers 6:24–26 was written on two small, silver amulets. Gabriel Barkay of Tel Aviv University placed the date of these during the First Temple period, between 960 BC and 586 BC. This again demonstrates that the Pentateuch was complete long before the supposed 400 BC threshold.*

Critics have also argued that Yahweh—the name for God—was not used before 500 BC–400 BC. If true, this would preclude Moses as the author of the Pentateuch. But the silver amulets contained the name Yahweh and were dated before 586 BC, which undercuts the assumption that the Pentateuch was not written by Moses or even in Moses' time.[8]

Critics have further claimed that the Hebrew moral code was too advanced to have been developed by 1200 BC. They say such an advanced social structure could not have come about before the 800s BC. Yet archaeology has uncovered the Akkadian Empire's Code of Hammurabi, dating to before 1200 BC. These laws parallel the laws of Moses, establishing that such advanced moral codes did indeed exist, not only during the time of Moses but prior to it as well.[9]

These findings and many others provide overwhelming evidence to support the view that Moses indeed wrote the entire Pentateuch.

Even though there is abundant evidence for the claim that the Bible is historically reliable, do we still need faith to believe the truths of the Bible? Why or why not?

_____

_____

_____

_____

_____

Why will there always be people who doubt God's Word and don't understand the meaning of his truth? Read 1 Corinthians 2:13–15.

_____

_____

_____

_____

Apply It This Week

This week, share with a friend or family member about the reliability of Scripture. Here are some conversation starters to help you:

- Some people say the disciples of Jesus made up the stories they wrote about in the New Testament. What do you think?

- I have been studying how reliable the Old and New Testament are in my small group. I've discovered. . .

In a devotional time before God, read Proverbs 2:1–9. The real answer to life comes from gaining understanding and wisdom from God. Write a prayer expressing your desire to be a seeker of wisdom and one who is in awe of the God who created you and loves you.

_____

_____

_____

_____

_____

_____

This week, before the next group meeting, read chapters 12–14 in *God-Breathed*. These chapters will further reinforce your faith in the God who has superintended the passing down of his reliable Word.

Close in Prayer

Pray that the truth you have encountered will become real, alive, and active in your life. Use this prayer time to express your desire to more deeply experience the power and relevance of God's Word.

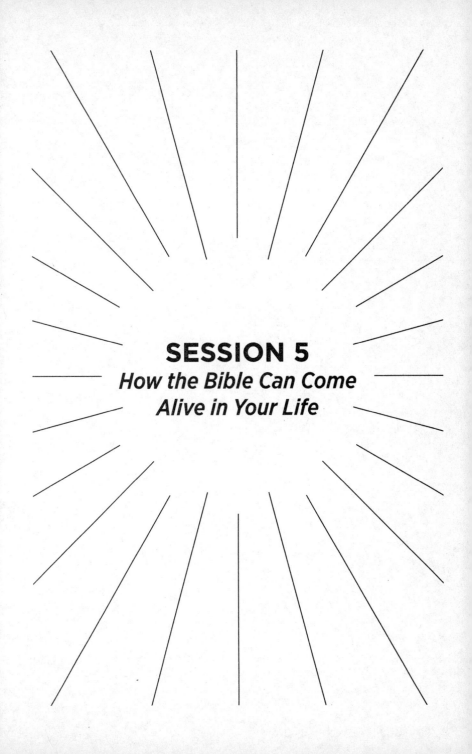

SESSION 5
How the Bible Can Come
Alive in Your Life

What Do You Think?

Growing from childhood to adulthood involves many different experiences—including being disciplined or corrected by your parents. When you were growing up, do you remember the voice of an inspecting dad or the disappointed tone of a distraught mother? Without disparaging your parents, share an experience that represents how you responded to being disciplined.

"I remember a time when. . ."

_____

_____

_____

_____

Session Objective

To discover a fresh and clear perception of the God of the Bible so that he and his truth can become more alive in our lives.

How Do You Respond?

Have someone in the group read aloud the following paragraphs, which are adapted from chapter 15 of *God-Breathed*.

> *"You come out here right now," the man commanded with a stern voice. When the child appeared, the father said, "I told you to clean up this garage, and it hasn't been touched. Why haven't you obeyed me?"*

> *Have you ever heard the voice of an inspecting dad or the disappointed tone of a distraught*

mother? Most of us grew up receiving correction for those things we didn't do properly. How that correction was handed out and how we received it can dramatically affect our sense of acceptance. And for many who experienced authoritative parents, that sense of acceptance naturally became performance based.

One of the biggest mistakes people make is reading the Bible through a distorted lens of past experiences. That approach skews our view of God and our relationship with him. Our perception of God is generally colored by our child-to-parent relationships, especially the child-to-father relationship. How you related to your parents has no doubt greatly influenced your perception of God. For example, if you grew up with authoritarian parents and felt their disapproval, you may tend to project those feelings into your relationship with God. It is natural to bring that distorted lens to your reading of Scripture, causing you to see God as an authoritarian and disapproving figure.

Through what type of lens do you tend to see Scripture? Answer the questions below and try to explain your answers.

1. When you read the Bible, how often do you ask yourself, "What sin here needs to be avoided?" (Circle your response below.)

    a. I seldom or never ask that.
    b. I sometimes ask that.
    c. I often or always ask that.

Do you tend to think that God is inspecting you or watching you critically? Why or why not?

_____

_____

_____

_____

_____

_____

2. When you read the Bible, how often do you ask yourself, "What commands here do I need to obey?" (Circle your response below.)

       a. I seldom or never ask that.
       b. I sometimes ask that.
       c. I often or always ask that.

Do you tend to see God as a demanding God who wants immediate obedience? Why or why not?

_____

_____

_____

_____

_____

_____

3. When you read the Bible, how often do you ask yourself, "What part of my life needs to change?" (Circle your response below.)

    a. I seldom or never ask that.
    b. I sometimes ask that.
    c. I often or always ask that.

Do you tend to view God as a disappointed God who requires perfect performance? Why or why not?

_____

_____

_____

_____

_____

_____

Have someone in the group read the following paragraphs aloud:

> *It is not that we shouldn't avoid sin or understand what biblical commands we need to obey. But when we view God's Word through the lens of a disappointed and inspecting God, we distort his truth. Paul told the Christ-followers in Ephesus that he was praying that God would "give you the Spirit of wisdom and revelation, so that you may know [Jesus] better. . .that the eyes of your heart may be enlightened in order that you may know the hope to which he has called you" (Ephesians 1:17–18 NIV).*

*In this passage, the Greek word for "wisdom"
is* ophia, *which refers to wisdom in spiritual
truth providing insight into the true nature of
things. The word "revelation" is from the Greek*
apokalupsis, *which means the uncovering or
unveiling of the knowledge of God to the soul. In
other words, when Paul prays that the eyes of our
hearts would be enlightened, he is asking God to
peel back the distorted view we have of God and
to let us see the true nature of who Jesus is until it
penetrates deep into our souls.*

*God wants to open the eyes of our hearts to see
him for who he is. He wants to purge our minds
and emotions of the false image of a disappointed
or inspecting God that may have been placed
there by past or present unhealthy relationships.
He wants his God-breathed words to cleanse and
rectify any distortions we may have of him. When
this is done, we can experience God as he meant us
to experience him.*

*One of the most effective ways for the Bible
to come alive in our lives is for us to gain a correct
view of an accepting Jesus. He wants to peel back
the distorted view that we tend to have of him as
being an inspecting or disappointed Jesus.*

Imagine journeying back in time to when Jesus was on earth.
You are assembled at the Passover meal with Jesus (the Last
Supper). The story is recorded in John 14. How you hear the
words of Jesus in the narrative is very telling.

Have someone in the group read John 14:15 aloud.

Imagine yourself seated across the table from Jesus. He looks your way, and you make eye contact with him as he says, "If you love me, you will keep my commandments." In your mind and in your emotions, how would you respond to his statement? Why would Jesus be saying these words to you? (Write your answer here and share it with the group.)

_____

_____

_____

_____

_____

_____

Have someone in the group read the following paragraphs aloud:

Is Jesus Disappointed?

Do you possibly hear Jesus' words through some past feeling of false guilt? Do you see Jesus crossing his arms and shaking his head, saying, "If you really loved me, you would have kept my commandments all along. Your failings before, and even now, speak volumes. I know you are trying to please me, but you are such a disappointment."

What do you hear in Jesus' voice as he makes his statement about love and commandments? If you sense his disappointment (however consciously or subliminally), you might compensate by working harder at performing for God in hopes of feeling worthy of his love. The problem is, no one can live the Christian life perfectly. If we sense in Scripture a disappointed God, we will tend to see his love as a reward for our good performance. This may cause us to see only the "thou shalt nots" of the Bible and miss its many promises. This view sets up our emotions to feel, I must do right to be loved right. *Invariably, this perception will affect all our relationships.*

Keep the Last Supper image in your mind. When you hear Jesus say, "If you love me, you will keep my commandments," do you see him raising his eyebrows and emphasizing the first word, "If"?

Do you hear a questioning tone in Jesus' voice, as if his statement were really something of a warning: "Do you know that I'm watching you to see if you keep my commandments?" (Write your answer here and share it with the group.)

_____

_____

_____

_____

_____

Have someone in the group read the following paragraphs aloud:

Is Jesus Inspecting You?

Some people see God as an inspector who grades us on how well we follow the directives in the Bible. Is that the kind of God you see? Is he one who

*stands over you with a pad and pencil, keeping a
running tally of all your deeds, both good and bad?
It's hard to imagine this kind of God celebrating
who you are or being happy just to be with you. His
scrutinizing, inspecting eye would sap the joy out of
the relationship.*

*If we see God as an inspector, we might tend to
take even the slightest corrective suggestion from
others as a personal attack and become defensive.
We also may be prone to take on the role of inspector
ourselves and suspiciously monitor the behavior
of others. We might make big deals out of minor
biblical issues. As you can imagine, people find
it difficult to enjoy the fellowship of someone
who keeps them under scrutiny and records any
deviation from the letter of the law.*

If you don't imagine Jesus as an inspector or as a disappointed
Jesus, how *do* you view him when he says, "If you love me, you
will keep my commandments"? (Write your answer here and
share it with the group.)

_____

_____

_____

_____

_____

Have someone in the group read the following paragraphs aloud:

Is Jesus Accepting of You?

When you hear Jesus' statement, do you perceive an accepting God? Do your eyes meet? This is your Savior, who sees you just the way you are and loves and accepts you beyond your wildest dreams. He tells you there are many rooms in his Father's house, and he is going to prepare a place for you. Then he makes you a promise: "I will come and get you, so that you will always be with me where I am" (John 14:3).

Jesus now explains that the works he has done were actually not of his own doing: it was the Father working through him. And he makes you another promise: "Anyone who believes in me will do the same works I have done" (John 14:12).

He smiles reassuringly and gives you yet another promise: "You can ask for anything in my name, and I will do it" (John 14:13). Do any of these promises sound like something coming from a disappointed or inspecting Jesus? They are coming from the One who welcomes you and receives you with a full embrace and without reservation or conditions. Then, in a tender voice with accepting eyes, he makes you a final promise. Listen to his words as he extends his arms toward you and with a smile on his face says, "If you love Me, you will keep My commandments" (John 14:15 NASB).

This is the beginning statement of a very special promise to you. It is meant to bring you reassurance, security, and confidence. Listen to the actual promise in the next two verses: "I will

ask the Father, and he will give you another
Advocate, who will never leave you. He is the
Holy Spirit, who leads into all truth" (John
14:16–17). Doesn't this give you incredible
confidence? In effect, Jesus is saying, "If you and
I have a loving relationship, I promise I am
not going to leave you alone to try to live the
Christian life in your own strength. I'm going to
take up residence in your life through the power
and person of my Holy Spirit, and I will be there
to empower you. I will be there to give you the
joy in life that I have always intended for you."
Remember, he adds, "I have told you this so that
my joy may be in you and that your joy may be
complete" (John 15:11 NIV).

This is the promise that comes to us from the
accepting Jesus. And when we embrace his
biblical promise, his love becomes real to us. In
fact, it is his transforming love that enables us to
love him back so deeply and to love each other as
Jesus loves us.

That is the God the Bible reveals. Receive his
unconditional acceptance and experience freedom
from false guilt and self-condemnation. Respond to
the welcoming embrace of the Savior and rest in his
secure arms. Reach out and grasp his promise and
be infused with his Holy Spirit, who empowers you
to live a life pleasing to him.[10]

If the God-breathed words of Scripture are to
come alive in our lives, we must see Jesus for who
he is—the God who loves and accepts us without

condition. He is there with outstretched arms,
longing to lead us through his Word so we can
know him more intimately.

Spend a few moments in quiet reflection and write how you want to see more clearly an accepting Jesus who loves you for who you are—mistakes and all. Share with the group what you've written.

_____

_____

_____

_____

_____

_____

Apply It This Week

This week, share with a friend or family member how God's Word is to come alive in our lives and how seeing an accepting God is vital in order for that to happen. Here are some conversation starters to help you:

- I've been involved in a study about the Bible and how we view God. Do you tend to see God as a rather stern God who demands obedience? Why or why not?

- Our small group has been discussing how we view God and the Bible this week. I've been learning. . .

In a devotional time before God, read Matthew 11:28–29. Write a prayer expressing your desire to be yoked—in close relationship—with Jesus so you can know him as the unconditionally accepting God who wants to empower you to be more like him.

_____

_____

_____

_____

_____

_____

This week, read chapter 15 in *God-Breathed*.

Close in Prayer

Pray that the truth you have encountered will become real, alive, and active in your life. Use this prayer time to express your desire to more deeply experience the power and relevance of God's Word.

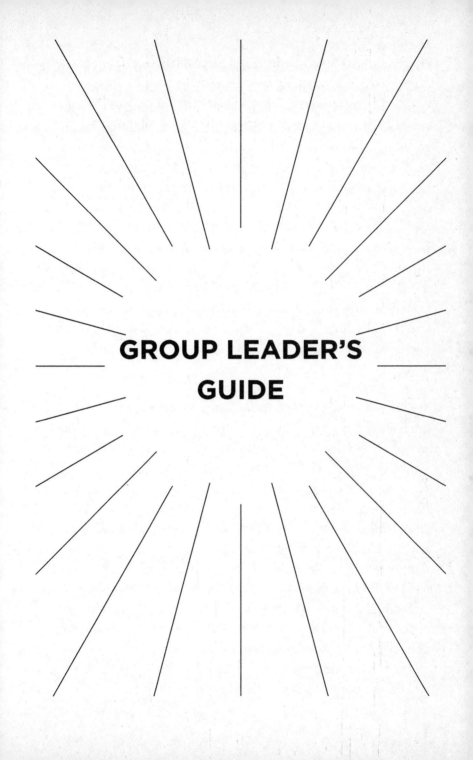

GROUP LEADER'S GUIDE

Purpose of This Study

Using the *God-Breathed Study Guide* with a small group means you will have approximately five hours of interaction with them. This study is designed for a one-hour period per session. It is based on the *God-Breathed* book by Josh McDowell. Drawing from the book, it encourages group participants to read certain chapters between sessions. This study, along with the companion book, communicates both the compelling message of how God's Word is alive and powerful and how it is accurate and reliable. As a result of this study your group participants will capture a sense of awe and mystery for the Bible which they may otherwise consider to be dull and hard to understand. The *God-Breathed* study can truly become a transformative time as each participant experiences the living and reliable truth of God's Word. "For the word of God is alive and powerful" (Hebrews 4:12).

How to Use the Study Guide

The *God-Breathed Study Guide* is designed to be used interactively by a group and by individuals as well. An individual can certainly benefit by going through it alone; however, more can be experienced and accomplished in a group context.

Each group participant needs a copy of the study guide. (The study guide is not intended to be shared by couples.) Order enough copies so each person attending your group can have one. They can be obtained through your local Christian supplier or by calling the publisher at 800-852-8010. Or go online to Barbour Publishing at www.barbourbooks.com. It is wise to order a few extra copies to cover individuals who may show up at later sessions. Your church may decide to provide the study guides, or you may want to ask each participant to contribute toward the purchase of their resources.

As stated earlier, the book *God-Breathed* is the companion to the study experience. You will want to encourage that each participant read a selection of chapters between sessions. However, no reading assignment is required prior to the first session. Couples can share in the reading of the book, so one book per couple is recommended. Consider adding this resource to your order of study guides. You may order the book from your local Christian supplier or by contacting Barbour Publishing as noted above.

Session Overview
Each session of this guide is divided into five areas:

What Do You Think?
This section includes a brief introduction to the session's subject and includes questions for interactive discussion by the group. Space is provided for note taking.

Session Objective
The objective identifies the desired outcome of the session.

How Do You Respond?
This is the main question-and-answer section with Scripture readings, readings provided from *God-Breathed*, and interactive questions to stimulate group discussion. The answers will come from your group's own knowledge and from an understanding of various readings featured in the session.

Apply It This Week
Here you encourage your group to share what they are learning with a friend or family member during

the week. A devotional Scripture and prayer time activity are provided, too. You will want to encourage participants to read the chapter assignments from *God-Breathed* as well. The particular chapters to read are referenced at the end of the Apply It This Week section.

Close in Prayer

While closing in prayer may seem like the expected thing to do, we encourage you to make praying together a very intentional exercise. Pray as a group that the truth you have encountered will become real, alive, and active in your lives throughout the week. Use your prayer time to express your desire to more deeply experience the power and relevance of God's Word. Praying together is an important part of making your group experience come alive.

Suggestions to Guide Your Discussion

Interacting with your group about the Bible is good, but healthy discussions are those that lead people to trust more deeply in the truth of God's Word and challenge them to live out those truths in their lives. Here are some suggestions to guide your group discussion to that end.

1. *Don't be afraid of silence.* Some group leaders make the mistake of asking a thought-provoking question and then, when no one answers immediately, moving on too quickly to the next question. Wise leaders create an atmosphere in which careful thought is encouraged through the judicious use of silence. Allow a brief time for thought after each question (if necessary), and signal for someone

to speak up by simply asking, "Anybody?" or "Someone finish your thought out loud."

2. *Let the discussion follow its own path without letting the group stray too far.* If the discussion is moving forward in a positive vein, don't be in a hurry to move to the next question in the study guide. But be careful not to let the discussion stray onto tangents not related to the topic.

3. *As often as possible, follow a comment with another question.* After a person has made an observation, ask, "Can you think of an example?" or ask how the rest of the group would respond.

4. *Don't feel obligated to ask all (or exclusively) the questions in the study guide.* If your group's time is limited, highlight the questions you wish to ask. Add questions suited to your own group as the discussion develops.

5. *When it's practical, "prime the pump" by planting questions with the most vocal or well-spoken participants.* If your group is slow to start discussions, jot one or two questions onto index cards and give them to some of your most vocal group members before the session, asking them to be ready to offer comments if others don't jump in quickly. You may also ask several confident individuals if they will allow you to call them by name to answer a question if the discussion begins to lag. But don't allow the vocal ones to dominate the discussion. Encourage everyone to participate.

6. *Seek attitudinal and behavioral responses.* Don't seek "right" answers as much as honest discussion. Don't just probe what your group thinks about a topic; ask how they respond attitudinally or behaviorally to the question. The idea is to search out where each person is on their spiritual journey. This isn't to say that wrong attitudes or actions should be agreed with or condoned; it simply means you are creating an atmosphere of transparency and safety where people can open up and be honest with God and with each other.

7. *Finally, refer frequently to Scripture as your baseline.* You will notice that Scripture passages are referred to liberally throughout this study guide. Though opinions may vary on a lot of issues, encourage your group to answer the question, "What is *God's* view of this issue?" In order for your participants to discover what God's position is, they must turn to his Word. Scripture is always our definitive source for revealing God's truth.

Your role as a group leader or facilitator is significant. May God use your gifts to his glory as you encourage your group to seek him and to allow his Word to come alive in their lives.

Notes

1. http://www.unitedbiblesocieties.org/what-we-do /distribution/.

2. Peter W. Flint, *The Dead Sea Scrolls*, (Nashville: Abingdon, 2013), 38.

3. Ibid., xx.

4. Ibid., xxi.

5. J. Harold Greenlee, *Introduction to New Testament Textual Criticism* (Grand Rapids: Eerdmans, 1977), 54.

6. Suetonius, *Life of Claudius in The Twelve Caesars*, trans. Robert Graves, revised by Michael Grant (New York: Viking Penguin, 1979), 25.4.

7. Flavius Josephus, *The Antiquities of the Jews* (New York: Ward, Lock, Bowden, 1900), 20.9.1.

8. Harold L. Willmington, *Willmington's Bible Handbook* (Wheaton, IL: Tyndale, 1997), 889.

9. "Archaeology and Sources for Old Testament Background," *New Living Translation Study Bible* (Wheaton, IL: Tyndale, 2008), 8.

10. Adapted from Josh and Sean McDowell, *Experience Your Bible* (Eugene, OR: Harvest House, 2012), 37–48.

About the Author

Over the past fifty years, Josh McDowell has spoken to more than 25 million people in 125 countries about the evidence for Christianity and the difference the Christian faith makes in the world. He has authored or coauthored more than 140 books (with more than 54 million copies in print), including such classics as *More Than a Carpenter* and *New Evidence That Demands a Verdict*. Josh and his wife, Dottie, have been married for more than forty-four years and have four grown children and ten grandchildren. They live in Southern California.

About the Writer

Dave Bellis is a ministry consultant focusing on strategic planning and product development. He is a writer, producer, and product developer. He and his wife, Becky, have two grown children and live in northeastern Ohio.